VIRGINIA

Laura Pratt

www.av2books.com

Go to **www.av2books.com**, and enter this book's unique code.

BOOK CODE

T346107

AV² by Weigl brings you media enhanced books that support active learning.

AV² provides enriched content that supplements and complements this book. Weigl's AV² books strive to create inspired learning and engage young minds in a total learning experience.

Your AV² Media Enhanced books come alive with...

Audio
Listen to sections of the book read aloud.

Video
Watch informative video clips.

Embedded Weblinks
Gain additional information for research.

Try This!
Complete activities and hands-on experiments.

Key Words
Study vocabulary, and complete a matching word activity.

Quizzes
Test your knowledge.

Slide Show
View images and captions, and prepare a presentation.

... and much, much more!

Published by AV² by Weigl
350 5th Avenue, 59th Floor
New York, NY 10118
Website: www.av2books.com   www.weigl.com

Library of Congress Cataloging-in-Publication Data
Pratt, Laura.
 Virginia / by Laura Pratt.
   p. cm. -- (Explore the U.S.A.)
 Includes bibliographical references and index.
 ISBN 978-1-61913-413-3 (hard cover : alk. paper)
 1. Virginia--Juvenile literature. I. Title.
 F226.3.P728 2012
 975.5--dc23
                    2012016585

Printed in the United States of America in North Mankato, Minnesota
1 2 3 4 5 6 7 8 9 16 15 14 13 12

052012
WEP040512

Project Coordinator: Karen Durrie
Art Director: Terry Paulhus

Weigl acknowledges Getty Images as the primary image supplier for this title.

VIRGINIA

Contents

3

This is Virginia.
It is the Old Dominion State.
This name came from
the king of England.

5

This is the shape of Virginia. It is in the east part of the United States.

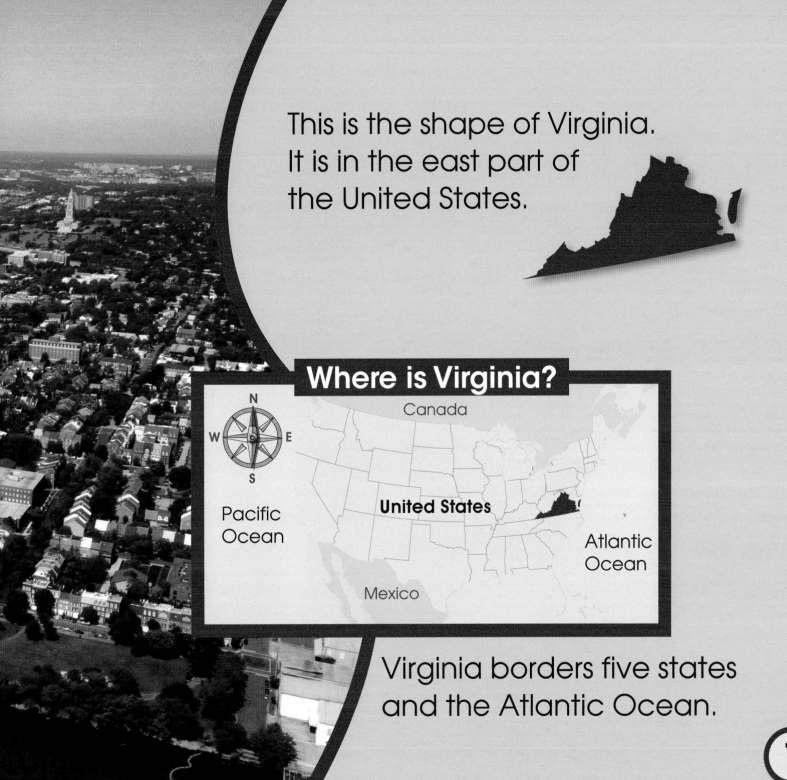

Where is Virginia?

Canada

N
W E
S

Pacific Ocean

United States

Atlantic Ocean

Mexico

Virginia borders five states and the Atlantic Ocean.

The first English town in North America was in Virginia. It was called Jamestown.

George Washington was born in Virginia.

The Virginia state flower is the dogwood. This is a kind of tree that grows flowers.

The seal of Virginia has a goddess in the middle.

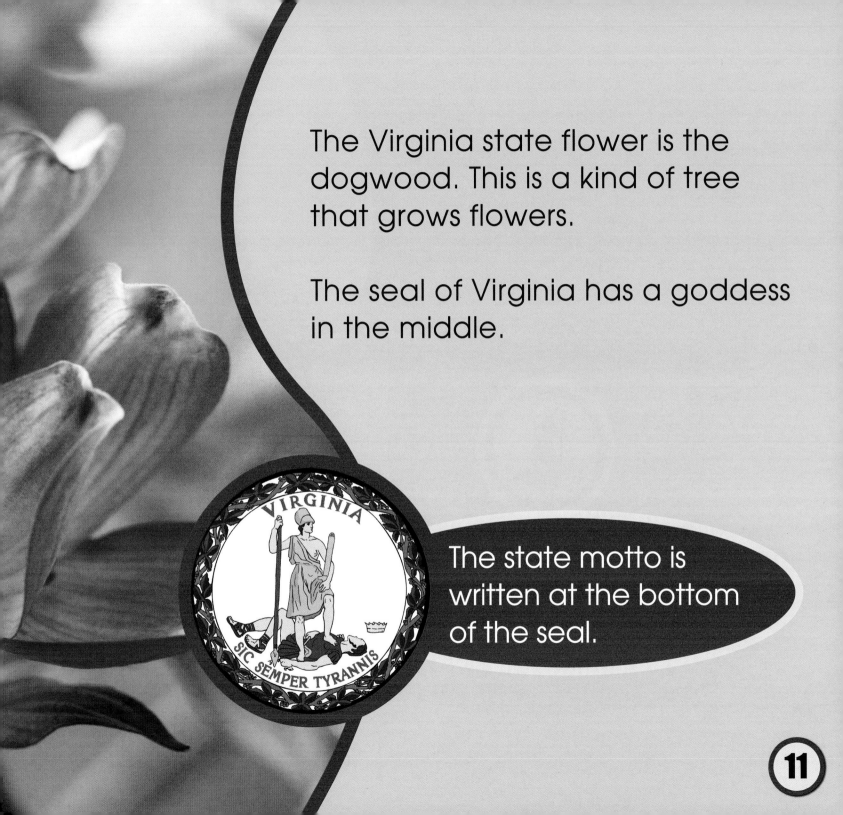

The state motto is written at the bottom of the seal.

This is the state flag of Virginia. It has the state seal against a blue background.

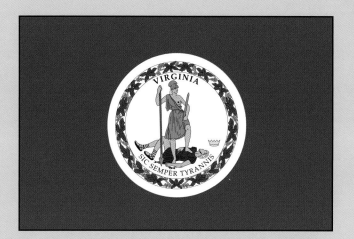

The state flag has not changed since 1861.

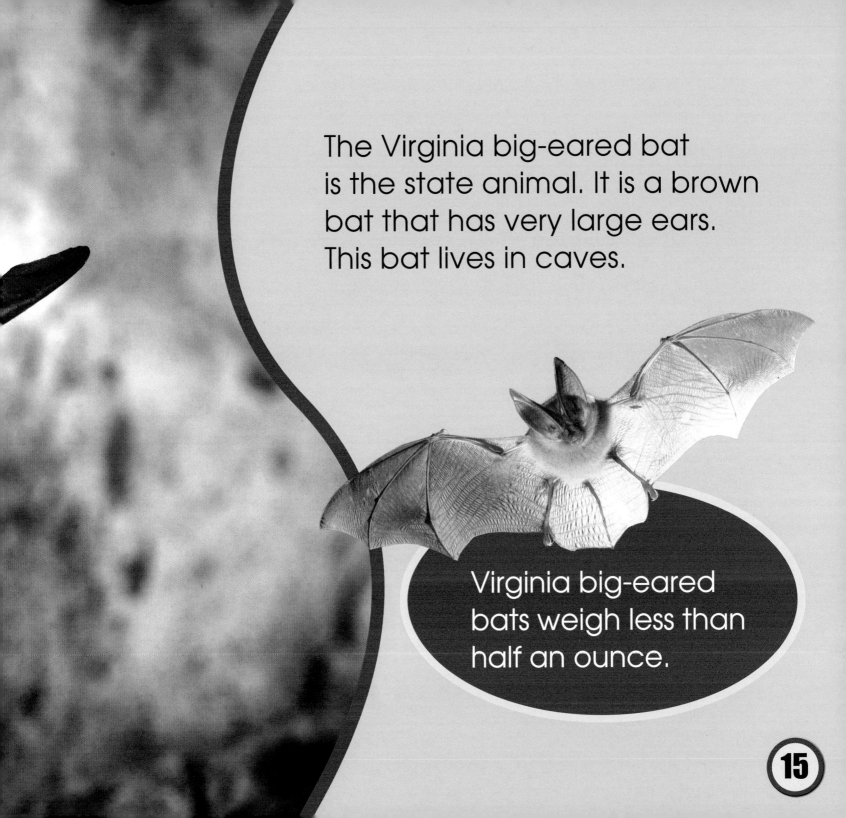

The Virginia big-eared bat is the state animal. It is a brown bat that has very large ears. This bat lives in caves.

Virginia big-eared bats weigh less than half an ounce.

This is Richmond. It is the capital city of Virginia. Richmond is next to the James River.

Thomas Jefferson designed the Virginia capitol building.

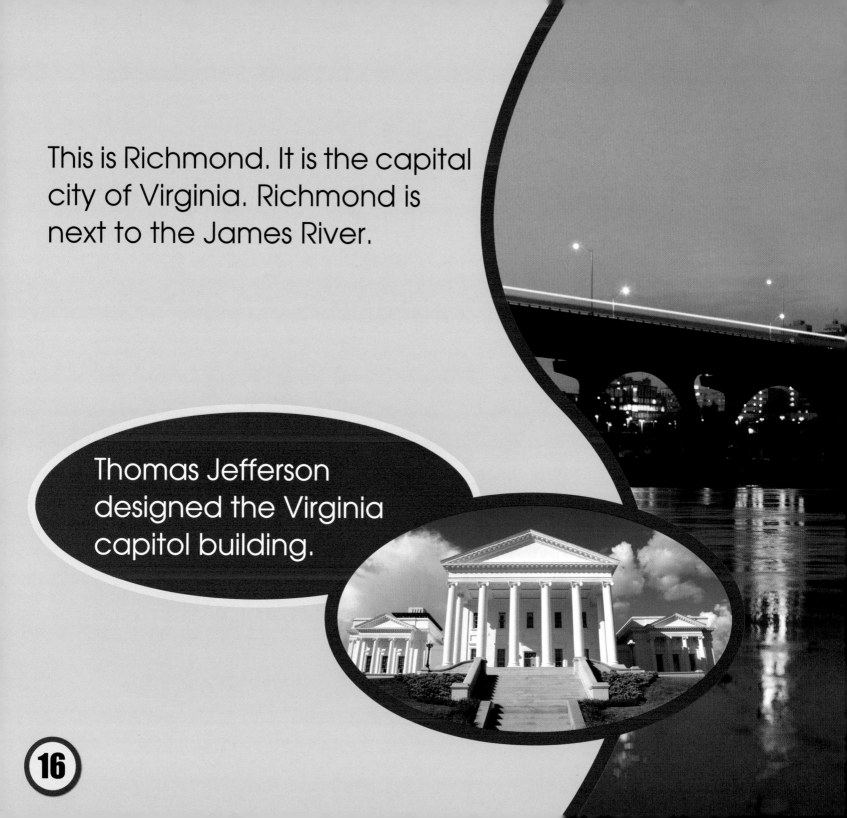

There are many dairy and egg farms in Virginia. Virginia dairy cows can make more than 1 billion pounds of milk in one year.

Chicken farming is also important in Virginia.

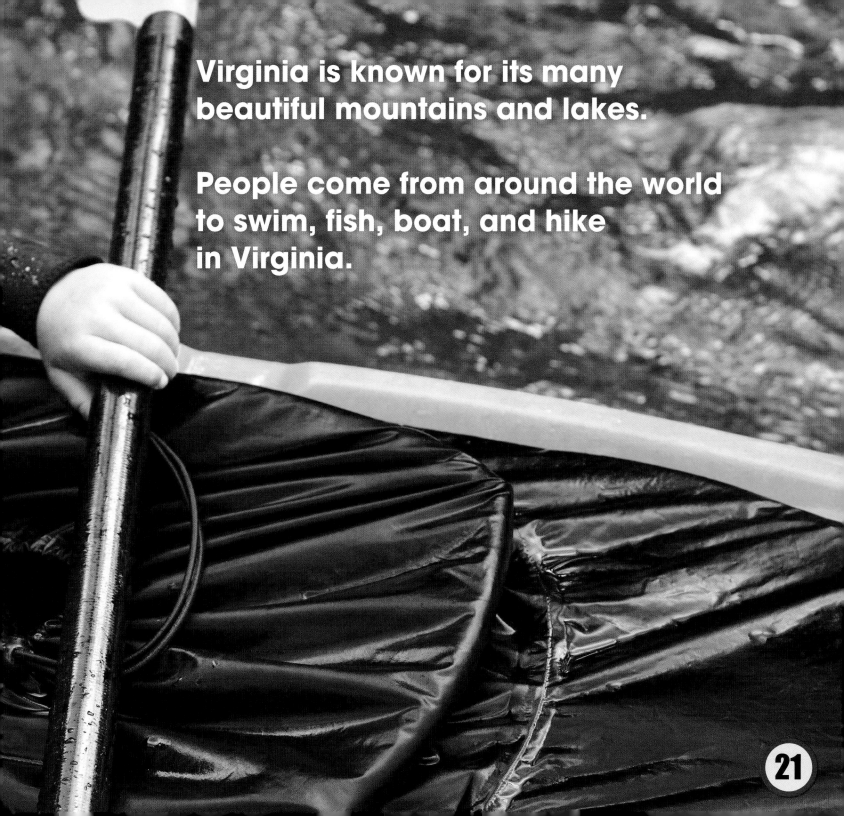

Virginia is known for its many beautiful mountains and lakes.

People come from around the world to swim, fish, boat, and hike in Virginia.

VIRGINIA FACTS

These pages provide detailed information that expands on the interesting facts found in the book. These pages are intended to be used by adults as a learning support to help young readers round out their knowledge of each state in the *Explore the U.S.A.* series.

Pages 4–5

Eight United States presidents were born in Virginia. This is more than in any other state. The first U.S. president, George Washington, was born in Virginia before the United States became a country. Other presidents born in Virginia are Thomas Jefferson, James Madison, James Monroe, William Henry Harrison, John Tyler, Zachary Taylor, and Woodrow Wilson.

Pages 6–7

On June 25, 1788, Virginia became the 10th state to join the United States. Virginia is bordered by Maryland and West Virginia to the north, Kentucky to the west, Tennessee and North Carolina to the south, and the Atlantic Ocean to the east. The Blue Ridge Mountains run through Virginia. These mountains are part of the Appalachian Mountain chain.

Pages 8–9

Virginia was one of the original 13 colonies that formed the United States. The state was named after Queen Elizabeth I of England. She was known as the Virgin Queen. British explorer Sir Walter Raleigh may have given Virginia its name around the year 1584. Virginia is officially called the Commonwealth of Virginia.

Pages 10–11

On Virginia's state seal, the goddess of virtue is dressed as a warrior. She holds a spear pointing down and a sword pointing up. Her left foot rests on the chest of the figure of tyranny, who is lying on the ground. Virtue represents Virginia, and the tyrant stands for Great Britain. The image symbolizes Virginia's triumph over Great Britain in the American Revolution.

KEY WORDS

Research has shown that as much as 65 percent of all written material published in English is made up of 300 words. These 300 words cannot be taught using pictures or learned by sounding them out. They must be recognized by sight. This book contains 53 common sight words to help young readers improve their reading fluency and comprehension. This book also teaches young readers several important content words, such as proper nouns. These words are paired with pictures to aid in learning and improve understanding.

Page	Sight Words First Appearance
4	came, from, is, it, name, of, old, state, the, this
7	and, in, part, where
8	first, was
11	a, at, grows, has, kind, that, tree
12	changed, not
15	an, animal, large, lives, than, very
16	city, next, to
19	also, are, can, farms, important, make, many, more, one, than, there, year
20	around, come, for, its, mountains, people, world

Page	Content Words First Appearance
4	dominion, England, king, Virginia
7	Atlantic Ocean, shape, United States
8	George Washington, Jamestown, North America, town
11	bottom, dogwood, flower, goddess, middle, motto, seal
12	background, flag
15	big-eared bat, ears, caves, ounce
16	building, James River, Richmond, Thomas Jefferson
19	cows, milk, pounds
20	lakes

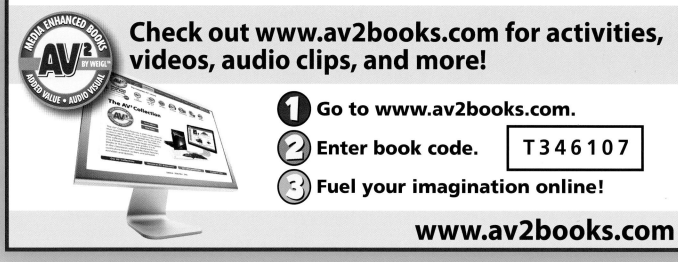

Check out www.av2books.com for activities, videos, audio clips, and more!

1 Go to www.av2books.com.

2 Enter book code. `T 3 4 6 1 0 7`

3 Fuel your imagination online!

www.av2books.com